Show me how to WITHDRAWN
MachineQuilt

A FUN, NO-MARK APPROACH

Kathy Sandbach

C&T PUBLISHING

Copyright © 2002 Kathy Sandbach

Editor: Beate Marie Nellemann
Technical Editor: Joyce Engels Lytle
Proofreaders: Stacy Chamness and Lucy Grijalva
Design Director/Book Designer: Christina D. Jarumay
Cover Designer: Christina D. Jarumay
Illustrations: Aliza Kahn Shalit
Quilt Photography: Mark Frey
How-to Photography: Steven Buckley, Photographic Reflections
Production Assistant: Kirstie L. McCormick

Library of Congress Cataloging-in-Publication Data
Sandbach, Kathy,
  Show me how to machine quilt : a fun, no-mark approach / Kathy Sandbach.
    p. cm.
Includes bibliographical references and index.
  ISBN 1-57120-128-9 (Paper trade)
  1. Machine quilting--Patterns. 2. Quilts. I. Title.
  TT835 .S263 2002
  746.46--dc21

                          2001003399

Published by C&T Publishing, Inc.
P.O Box 1456
Lafayette, California 94549

Printed in China
10 9 8 7 6 5 4 3 2 1

DEDICATION

It is only right to dedicate this book to all those customers who have let me "practice" my craft and skills on their quilts. Your trust in my ideas, technical skills, and artistry made this book possible.

ACKNOWLEDGMENTS

Many people—students, customers, shop owners, seminar directors, and friends—have helped make this book possible. A very special thanks to my sister, Maggie Hall, for her help from the beginning proposal to completion. Without her help in piecing, basting, testing, proofing, and encouragement this book would not have happened.

A warm thanks goes to Diana McClun, whose encouragement through the years has helped my confidence and artistic growth immeasurably. She said one day: "You need to do a book," and her steadfast friendship and gentle push have helped to make it happen.

Particular thanks to Laura Nownes, Margaret J. Miller, and Freddy Moran for their willingness to let me "do my thing" on their pieces over the years. What great fun to have such lovely pieces on which to hone my skills.

A very special thanks to everyone who helped by making quilts for this book—whether they ended up in print or not, your interest and time is very much appreciated… especially Denise, Kathleen, and members of the TLC Group in Lodi, California.

A huge share of gratitude goes to the folks at C&T Publishing, especially Beate Nellemann, my editor, for helping put this together. You folks are the greatest, and I am honored to be a part of the author family you encourage and promote.

TABLE OF Contents

Introduction

If you have found yourself with quilt tops galore and no time to quilt them, you've come to the right place. If you have tried marking quilt tops, getting just the right template or making a template just the right size, and figuring out how to mark, where to mark, and what to use to mark, you have the right book in hand! The main reason most of us make and quilt quilts, wall hangings, and art-to-wear garments is for **fun!** I have yet to meet anyone who enjoys the marking process—from finding the right design to getting rid of the marks that still show after the quilting is completed. The idea with this book is to eliminate the marking process and add immeasurably to the "fun" factor. Get rid of the idea that all quilting designs have to be "perfect" to look wonderful. Once you get the basics down, your workstation set up, and practice a bit, you can quilt anything!

Really! Eliminating the marking will save big chunks of time—and who has an excess of that these days? Not to mention that it will make the entire project more fun. Begin to think about what you might want to quilt as you are piecing or appliquéing the top. Soon you will look at open spaces as another place for a fun quilted design, rather than agonizing over what template you have that might fit that spot.

Most of the quilts we are making fall into one of five categories. These are discussed throughout the book. You can use the designs in this book for each category and then easily graduate to experimenting with designs of your own. Begin here and now to think of your sewing machine needle as a "pencil" with which to "draw," or better yet "sketch." Sketching lines somehow need to be less "perfect" to look good. Quilting

a double line of stitches will look more like sketching and neither line needs to be perfect! Machine quilting is my living—I work at the sewing machine most of every day. I try to quilt each piece that comes my way differently. Some designs are used again and again, but in a different size, shape, or cluster. You won't need much practice to use the designs shown here to stretch your creativity and increase your "fun factor."

The projects include diagrams of how I quilted each quilt. You can quilt yours the same way or any way you choose. At the back of the book are quilting designs, broken down into rows the way they are stitched, and include arrows for direction. Most are two rows, some are three. I suggest you "play" on a practice kit first, and practice the motion before graduating to the piece you may have spent months piecing. I find that most of the time the first row is very easy and I can quilt it simply pushing the sandwich through the machine away from me. Then to quilt the second row, I'll turn the piece sideways so I can "see" the form in its natural, upright state rather than trying to quilt backwards.

Use the troubleshooting suggestions from Chapter 5 on each project you complete, and you will be able to eliminate most of the problems that occur in making quilts. Your project will lie flat, hang perfectly straight, and generally look wonderful.

I hope you enjoy the process of machine quilting without marking, and don't forget that none of it has to be perfect to look **great!**

CHAPTER 1

Basic Tools

Machine quilting is great fun once you get started, but you need to start with the right tools. They'll help make your whole project a success with the least amount of frustration. I suggest you take a bit of time and set up your workstation, get your machine set, assemble the proper equipment, and then the project will be fun!

Sewing Machine

Success in machine quilting starts with a sewing machine in excellent working order. Having your machine freshly serviced with the timing in perfect adjustment will help your quilting stitches look good on both the top and backside of your quilt. You don't need a fancy machine, but it helps if your machine can drop its feed dogs to help you with free-motion quilting, and the larger the opening the machine has to the right of the needle the easier it will be to manipulate large quilts. If you're in the market for a new sewing machine, consider these two points.

Sewing Machine Feet

For free-motion quilting, you **must** have a darning foot for your machine. They come in many sizes and shapes. If you need to purchase one, make sure that you have the correct one for your machine. It's a good idea to test it at the shop before taking it home.

Darning feet

For simple straight-line quilting you will need a walking or even-feed foot for your machine. This foot "pushes" the top layer of fabric through the presser foot at the same rate that the feed dogs push the bottom layer. This is not an item that is generally included in the box of attachments but looks similar to the ones pictured. It is also imperative to use a walking foot for attaching the binding.

Walking feet

Needles

A very sharp needle, the correct size, is a **must** for successful machine quilting. The size of the needle depends on the thread that you are using. Most of the decorative and metallic threads will require a needle that is larger than the one used for piecing. A top-stitch needle will work very well in most machines; or use a jeans or denim needle, or a quilting needle. These are all **very** sharp, strong needles and have a pointed end rather than a "ball" or rounded tip such as a universal needle.

*Most of the problems with thread breakage, metallic threads shredding, or missed stitches come from not having the correct size needle in the machine. When you have a problem, check the needle first! Usually a **larger** needle will eliminate the problem.*

Experiment with different needles to find the right one for your machine and the right one for the project. I would suggest you keep a small notebook next to your machine and keep track of which needle works with which thread. This will eliminate needing to experiment and test each time you use a particular thread.

General Guidelines for Needles
- 60/8–70/10 for clear nylon and clear polyester
- 80/12–90/14 for sewing weight thread, size 50 weight cottons, and polyesters
- 100/16–110/18 for decorative threads including metallic, 30 and 40 weight rayon

Workstation

To help you manipulate the quilt under the machine needle, you need a large work surface. This means space for the quilt to lie without being pulled in any direction while you are quilting. Suggestions for the perfect work surface would include a backstop to keep the quilt from falling off the back of the table and a breadboard or pullout on your left to support the quilt bulk. A card table or other small surface can also be used to help support the quilt.

A word here about your sitting position: Sit as low as possible and look straight ahead rather than down on your work. It is much easier on your neck and shoulders and though it may take some getting used to, it will really help you in the long run. Try lowering your pneumatic chair a little at a time over a few weeks and you'll get used to the new position without really noticing a big change.

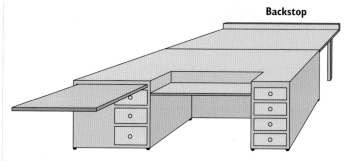

On the end can be a bookcase, or a double set of drawers in the front.
An ideal workstation setup

The large Plexiglas® table surround that is currently available is also an excellent support for the basic domestic machine if all you presently have is a free-arm style platform.

The larger your quilt the more difficult it is to manipulate under the needle. Rolling the bulk along the right edge seems to be the easiest way to control the bulk. Make sure that your hands rest on the flat surface of the quilt top rather than on top of the rolled bulk.

Threads

When machine quilting began its recent surge in popularity in the mid-1980s we were using clear or smoke-colored nylon to achieve a "hand quilted" look. As machine quilting gained acceptance and increased in popularity, the regular cotton threads and decorative threads have soared in popularity. My own thread stash now has many more decorative threads than regular ones.

Machines "like" the same thread in the top and the bobbin, but if you are using a rayon or metallic in the top, you probably **don't** want that in the bobbin. My own plan is to use a thread of equal **strength** in the bobbin and, if possible, the same color. For example: when using gold metallic on top, I'll use a Jeans gold cotton or polyester in the bobbin. By using the same color in the top and bobbin, the thread from the bobbin won't show on the top and the top thread won't show on the back if the free-motion movement should pull the thread to one side or the other.

With the wonderful array of threads available to quilters now, it is sometimes hard to pick the perfect one for your project. I always lean toward a variegated thread, if possible, when the fabric colors allow, as it is so much more interesting and eye-catching than a solid. YLI® cotton variegated threads are my favorites. A word of caution about the variegated threads: be careful when choosing them if your quilting design must be completely visible to look great because sometimes a particular color of the variegated range will "disappear" on the fabric of the same color and your design will be lost. If you are uncertain about the effect a certain thread will create, be sure to test it on a scrap of fabric. Of course, if you want your design to **really** show, use a very high contrast thread.

On many of the quilts I do, I change threads three or four (or more) times. Don't be afraid to try different threads on the same piece. Sometimes the whole piece won't look good with metallic, but some metallic will look great with other parts quilted in cotton thread.

Thread Tension Adjustment

You may have to adjust the tension on your machine if you are using unusual threads on your quilt: metallic, rayon, nylon, etc. Most of the time you can just adjust the top tension. Generally, the smaller the number on the tension dial the looser the tension, the larger the number the tighter the tension. Quilt a sample using the decorative threads to make sure the tension is correct. You don't want to see the top thread on the under side of the quilt, or the bobbin thread on the top of the quilt.

Bobbin tension is a bit trickier to adjust but once you get the hang of it, it really is simple. For those machines with a removable bobbin case, you will need to loosen or tighten the large screw. Hold the bobbin case with the closed side of the case facing right. Turn the screw right and it will be tighter, turn it left and it will be looser. This is easy to remember and since you will probably only have to turn it a small bit, maybe a quarter turn, it is easy to reset to its original position.

If your bobbin case is not removable, refer to your book of instructions or your sewing machine dealer to see how to adjust the bobbin tension. **You want the loosest tension possible while still getting a good stitch.**

Turn right to tighten, left to loosen.

Adjusting bobbin tension

❀ *Tip* *Choose a printed fabric rather than a solid color for your backing and small imperfections in the stitch tension or stitch size won't be noticeable. Using a wonderful busy print on the back allows bobbin thread changes to go almost unnoticed.*

"Fingers" or Gloves

While doing free-motion quilting your hands act as a "hoop." I use the same position for my hands for all free-motion work, as well as quilting with the walking foot. Your hands need to hold the fabric sandwich taut but not stretched. Rubber fingers from a stationery store, or quilter's gloves, will help hold the fabric taut and help you guide it smoothly. This will eliminate pleats or tucks on both the back and the top. I use rubber fingers on the middle and the index fingers of both hands, but many quilters prefer other methods of stabilizing the fabric sandwich. **It is very important to remember that your hands are guiding the fabric and keeping it taut at the same time**—just as a hoop would. See more about hand position in Chapter 3, page 11.

❀ *Tip* *If you see a "fullness" developing ahead of the needle, use your fingers to gently push the fabric toward the needle and ease in the fullness rather than letting a pleat develop.*

Fabrics and Batting

Fabrics

Virtually any fabric can be machine quilted. Fabric content (and quilting thread content) is no longer the huge concern it was a few years ago. The all-cotton rule seems to have disappeared around the time many of our quilts started hanging on the wall instead of lying on the bed. Silk, polyester, rayon, cotton, linen, and other specialty fabrics machine quilt beautifully. In other words, feel free to use any fabric you want in a piece you will machine quilt.

Backing fabric choices impact the total look of the quilt. To help the "felting" of the layers, it is best if the back is all cotton. With the choices available, and especially the many decorator fabrics that are 100% cotton, you have hundreds from which to choose. A large, busy print with many colors will allow you to change top thread and bobbin thread colors many times and still have a wonderful-looking quilt back.

Tip *Remember that if you plan to wash the quilt after it is completed, **all** the fabrics should be pre-washed, including the backing fabric.*

Batting

Batting choice is very important for a machine-quilted piece. The easiest batt to use is cotton. Cotton batt "felts" the layers of the quilt, almost eliminating shifting and helping to avoid pleats or tucks in the quilting on both front and back.

Warm and Natural® is my personal favorite for all machine quilting. It is very stable and lies perfectly flat every time, as it has not been scrunched into a bag that sometimes creates thin and thick spots or "waves."

Warm and Natural is a low-loft batting that is easy to roll and push through the machine. There are many other excellent battings on the market today that are 100% cotton, or mostly cotton, which will also give excellent results.

The larger your piece, the more bulk will become a consideration. Rolling your quilt up and pushing it through the machine becomes more difficult with a high loft or thick batting. Experiment with different battings on smaller pieces before trying to quilt a really large (queen size or larger) quilt. Even small amounts of loft multiply quickly when a large piece is rolled.

Polyester battings can be used, although the layers tend to shift, and the bulk of their loft can become a real problem. Mountain Mist Quilt Lite® is a very thin, low-loft polyester batt that works reasonably well for machine-quilting. But as with any polyester batting, the "felting" quality is lost completely.

The all-cotton and cotton/polyester battings will give a "flat," old-fashioned appearance to your quilt that many quilters want today, especially if the quilt is going to hang on a wall. Cotton battings will "block" very well, while polyester battings **do not** block at all! See Chapter 4, page 13, for specific directions on blocking.

Tip *Small pieces of cotton batting will sew together nicely on the machine if what you have isn't big enough for your project. Use the walking foot, the longest stitch, and widest zigzag stitch on your machine. Make sure that you have cleanly cut both edges with a rotary cutter before sewing. Butt the pieces together, don't overlap them, and carefully feed both pieces into the sewing machine.*

CHAPTER 3

Getting Ready to Quilt

Basting

The most important part of the preparation for quilting is the basting. Good basting will eliminate pleats forming on both the top and the back. Follow these guidelines carefully for consistently good results.

▪ Make sure that the back is **freshly** pressed!

▪ Spread the back face down on a hard flat surface. Using masking tape, tape the entire perimeter of the backing, starting in the middle of opposite sides and working out to outer edges. Make sure that the surface is taut and smooth **but not** stretched.

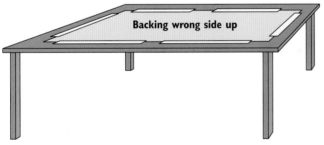

Taped backing

▪ Lay the batting on top of the backing, smoothing it flat. Place the quilt top on the batting, smoothing it flat and gently patting down any fullness that may have occurred in the piecing.

▪ Baste the entire surface with safety pins. Basting for machine quilting **cannot** be done with thread because removal of thread basting will break the machine quilting stitches. Place pins 4" to 6" apart in each direction.

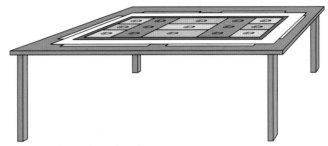

All three layers basted with pins.

▪ Remove the tape and trim the edges of the batting and backing down to about an inch outside the edge of the quilt top. This will eliminate as much of the bulk as possible and make pushing the quilt through the machine easier.

❀ *Tip Use Size 0 brass safety pins—they are by far the easiest to open and close. Try to pin around any pure white fabric areas as they could leave a tiny mark. I suggest* ***never*** *using any pin larger than a Size 1 as they have the potential to break threads and leave actual holes in your fabric.*

Quilting

Grid quilting is the first step. I always "grid quilt" before doing any of the decorative quilting. This means that all the "ditches" (seams) that need quilting are done first in both directions.

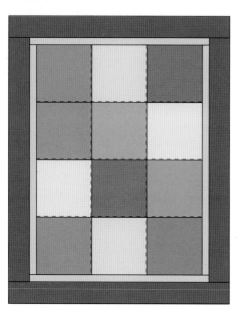

Ditch-quilt the body before the borders.

❀ *Important* While quilting, be careful that the top does not move and create pleats. Use your rubber fingers (or gloves) to carefully push any accumulating bulk toward the needle as you stitch, working in bits of fullness if there are any. If there is fullness in a block, make sure it stays in that block—don't let it get pushed to another area and distort the whole quilt. This applies when using either the walking foot or the darning foot.

Quilting compresses the layers and shrinks the entire project and allows you to work in fullness without creating pleats. Because of this shrinkage, however, it is important that you evenly quilt your pieces. Basically, a piece distorts if you do light and very heavy quilting on the same project. Evenly quilting your quilt will improve the overall appearance as well as helping the quilt hang nicely.

❀ *Tip* *If you are using stippling or meander quilting, or any very close quilting, do it **last**. This kind of quilting will shrink the piece noticeably and make the surrounding areas very full and puffy and much more difficult to quilt.*

Starts and Stops

This is a very important detail to make the quilting durable and secure through washing and handling. I use and recommend a small set of backstitches. Essentially, I begin quilting by first taking one complete stitch, pulling the bobbin thread up to the top. This beginning is about $1/4$" away from where I actually want the quilting to start; and then I stitch back to the start spot using regular length stitches and then come forward and stitch over the top of those stitches. Do this in a place where the thread matches the fabric, if possible, to camouflage the stitches. This is a much more secure beginning and ending than just a bunch of small stitches in a row. Finish by backing up over the top of the final $1/4$".

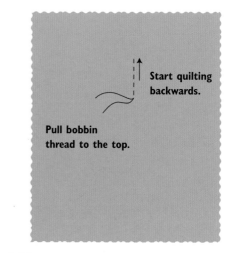

Start quilting backwards.

Pull bobbin thread to the top.

Backstitching

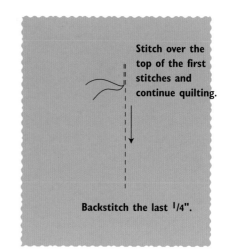

Stitch over the top of the first stitches and continue quilting.

Backstitch the last $1/4$".

Note Judges in any quilt competition require all starts and stops not to detract from the overall appearance of the quilting.

Hand Position

Even after quilting dozens of quilts, my hand position remains the same. **I do not reposition my hands while the machine is in motion!** By using the "U" position for hands, you can maintain both the tautness and control of the quilt. Keep your thumb tips together and only quilt within this five to six inch space. When the needle comes too close to your fingers, STOP the machine and re-position your hands. This is a bit tricky to get used to but easily mastered and will give your quilting lines a smooth line of continuity.

Notice the "U" shape position of the hands

Tip *If you have the "needle down" feature on your machine, use it! This helps secure the piece when you re-position your hands. Otherwise you need to move one hand at a time so the piece doesn't move on its own.*

Stitch Length

Your goal is an approximate stitch length of 10-12 stitches per inch. When you are first using the darning foot, you will probably need some practice to get the stitches even in length. If you move the piece too fast, you'll have only four stitches per inch—too slow and you'll have sixty or so stitches per inch. With just a little practice, you can get even-length stitches.

For easy curves or straight line stitching, you can use the walking foot and the machine will automatically take the correct number of stitches per inch. When you use the darning foot **you** guide the piece under the needle and you'll need to practice to get even-length stitches.

CHAPTER 4

Finishing the Quilt

Binding

The binding finishes off a quilt and is a **very** important part of the overall appearance. Here are some guidelines for perfect binding:

▮ Cut the binding on the cross grain of fabric—selvage to selvage. Exception to this would be a curved-edge quilt where a bias cut would be mandatory or a plaid or striped binding fabric that you wanted to cut on the bias.

▮ Approximate width should be 2" to 2 $^1/_2$".

▮ Be sure to piece the strips on the diagonal.

▮ Press in half lengthwise.

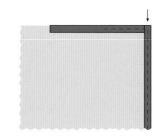

d *Now fold the piece down even with the cut edge of the quilt and begin to sew at the edge of the fold.*

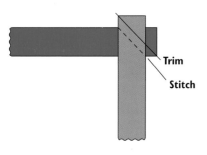

a *Piecing the binding on the diagonal.*

▮ Pull **slightly** on the binding as you sew it on. This will "gather in" the small amount of fullness on the borders that sometimes occurs with machine quilting.

▮ Make perfect mitered corners.

▮ Seam the beginning and ending pieces on the diagonal.

▮ Trim the quilt batting and backing to fill, but not "over stuff," the binding.

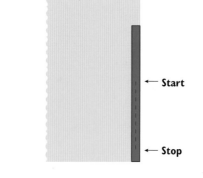

b *Leave a 6" tail. Begin sewing in the middle of a side; stop stitching $^1/_4$" from the corner and backstitch.*

c *Turn the quilt counter-clockwise and fold the binding up, away from the corner.*

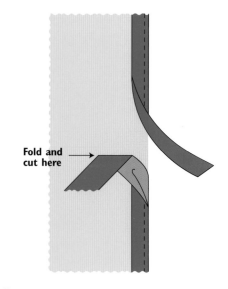

e *Sew the binding to all four sides and stop sewing about 8" from beginning. Pull it away from the machine and open the beginning tail and fold to the left at a right angle and cut it on the fold.*

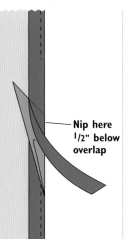

Nip here ¹/₂" below overlap

f *Refold beginning tail and lay ending tail over the top of it, and cut a small nip in the binding ¹/₂" beyond where it overlaps the beginning binding.*

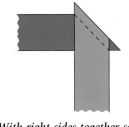

Fold and cut here

g *Open the ending tail and fold, at a 90° angle to the right, at the nip. Cut on the fold.*

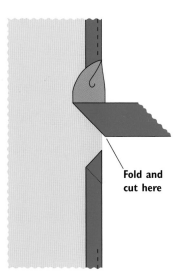

h *With right sides together sew the two binding edges together.*

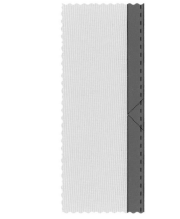

i *Refold binding in half and sew the remaining edge to the quilt.*

Back of Quilt

j *Whipstitch binding by hand to the back, tacking the mitered corners down.*

Sleeve

The best way to hang a quilt on the wall is to attach a sleeve to the back at the top. Cut the fabric 9" wide and piece if necessary with a ¹/₄" seam. Double fold and hem both short ends. Press in half lengthwise and sew to the top back after you've attached the binding by machine to the quilt front. Fold and whipstitch the binding to the back to cover the raw edges of both the quilt and the sleeve. Whipstitch the folded edge of the sleeve to the quilt back, making sure that you don't stitch through to the top of the quilt.

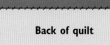
Top

Back of quilt

Attaching a sleeve

Blocking

This step is **very important**! The blocking of a quilt, especially a machine quilted piece, can make a huge difference in its overall appearance and in the way it hangs. There are two ways to block a quilt.

Wet Blocking

After the piece is entirely finished, including binding, you're ready to block the quilt. I block by laying a flat flannel sheet on a carpeted floor, placing the quilt on top of the flannel. The carpet helps to felt the layers and hold the piece in position. Spray the quilt with water until the top and batting are wet, but not soaked. The backing doesn't really get wet. Push the quilt into perfect shape with your hands, measure top, bottom and sides to make sure it is square and then let it dry **completely**. It will be perfect!

Steam Blocking

Again, when the piece is entirely finished, lay the quilt on a flat surface with a flannel sheet underneath and steam it with your iron. (I **don't** recommend doing this on a carpeted surface as the heat of the iron could damage the carpet.) **Don't press** the quilt, just lightly steam it. This is not as good a method as wetting the piece, but if you aren't sure about some of the fabric colors migrating or bleeding, it is the only sure way not to damage your piece.

✿ Tip *You can add as much as an inch or a bit more to the side of an uneven quilt with blocking, just by wetting it and gently stretching the short side and using T-pins to pin it to the carpet to hold it in place until it is totally dry.*

CHAPTER 5

Basic Hints and Troubleshooting

The Six "B's" of Quilting

Quilting during the last ten years, I have seen almost every problem we encounter as quiltmakers. Here are some hints to make your project as perfect as you possibly can.

Borders: You **cannot** simply sew strips or pieced borders to the body of the quilt!!! This adds fullness (extra fabric) and creates rippling fabric on the edges. You need to **measure** the body of the quilt and then measure the border pieces. Without careful measuring you will add fullness to the edges of the quilt.

Backing: If you need to piece your backing, be sure you measure the fabrics and pin them together before sewing them. If you just sew two big strips you will have fullness in one piece. It's the same principle as the borders. (Note: Remove the selvages before you sew pieces together. Cut, don't tear, them off.)

Batting: This was discussed earlier, but successful machine quilting starts with a first-quality **cotton** batting.

Basting: Careful basting will help keep your quilt tuck free and flat for perfect hanging or display.

Binding: Discussed in Chapter 4 in detail, but it is **very** important to the total look of the quilt to have the binding done correctly. Cut it cross grain, do all piecing diagonally, miter the corners, and pull slightly when attaching it to the quilt.

Blocking: Discussed in Chapter 4, but this is the single most important thing you can do to make your quilt lie flat, hang straight, and generally look wonderful. Make sure to use a flannel sheet as this "felts" the piece and lets you shape it perfectly!

CHAPTER 6

Projects and Designs

After quilting hundreds of quilts, I have found that about ninety-five percent of what quilters are piecing or appliquéing falls into one of five categories.

These include:
- Flora—including flowers, leaves, trees, bushes, plants, etc.
- Stars and/or Patriotic—all the star designs, plus patriotic themes
- Water—ocean, waves, boats, fish, and other aquatic things
- Children's—alphabet, baby, or kid's projects
- Holidays—Christmas, Halloween, etc.

I have developed a number of designs in each category that are all easy to do, and **do not** need to be marked. Most of the designs can be "chained together" or grouped, or will stand alone. The other five percent of quilts would be "art" quilts and many of these fall into one or more of the categories.

The following are five projects, one in each category, for you to try— simple piecing and/or fusible appliqué. The quilting designs I used are included.

Poppin' Poppies, 47" square, designed, pieced, and quilted by the author.

Fabrics

Background—2 ¼ yards

Narrow stripe for inner borders and binding—¾ yard

Bright orange for large petals and small flowers— ¾ yard

Light orange for small petals and small flower centers—
  ¼ yard

Three greens for leaves and center of large flower—
  total of ⅓ yard

Lightweight fusible webbing—2 yards if 18" wide

Backing—2 ½ yards

Cotton batting—approximately 51" square

Appliqué

All appliqué is done with lightweight fusible webbing. All the designs need to be enlarged 195%. Trace the designs on the paper side of the webbing and cut the shapes out roughly, leaving a ¼" or so outside the lines. Then fuse them on to the wrong side of the fabric and cut out exactly on the lines. Now peel the paper off the designs and fuse them onto the background fabric. I use the quilting to anchor the appliqué pieces, but you can buttonhole stitch them if you want.

Cutting

For ease of construction, the borders are added to the sides first, then the top and bottom. The cutting instructions will be different if you choose to miter the borders. Refer to your favorite basic quilt book.

Background

Cut a 24 ½" square centerpiece.

Cut four 4 ½"-wide strips from the length of fabric, then cut two 25 ½"-long strips and two 33 ½"-long strips for second border.

Cut four 7"-wide strips from the length of fabric, then cut two 34 ½"-long strips and two 47 ½"-long strips for the outside border.

Narrow Stripe

Cut eight 1"-wide strips, then from four of the strips, cut two 24 ½"-long strips and two 25 ½"-long strips for the first border. From the remaining strips, cut two 33 ½"-long strips and two 34 ½"-long strips for the third border.

Cut five 2 ½"-wide strips for binding.

Bright Orange

Cut 9 large petals and 16 small flowers.

Light Orange

Cut 9 small petals.

Cut 16 small circles for small flower centers.

Greens

Cut 21 leaves and 2 larger circles for center flower.

Piecing

1. Sew the 24 ½"-long narrow stripe strips to the opposite sides of center square. Always press the narrow stripe towards itself. Sew the 25 ½"-long narrow stripe strips to the top and bottom of the center square. Press.

2. Sew the 4 ½" x 25 ½" background strips to opposite sides of the quilt. Press toward the narrow stripe. Sew the 4 ½" x 33 ½" background strips to the top and bottom of the quilt. Press toward the narrow stripe.

3. Sew the 33 ½"-long narrow stripe strips to the opposite sides of the quilt. Press toward the narrow stripe. Sew the 34 ½"-long narrow stripe strips to the top and the bottom of the quilt. Press.

4. Sew the 7" x 34 ½" background strips to the sides of the quilt. Press toward the narrow stripe. Sew the 7" x 47 ½" background strips to the top and bottom of the quilt. Press.

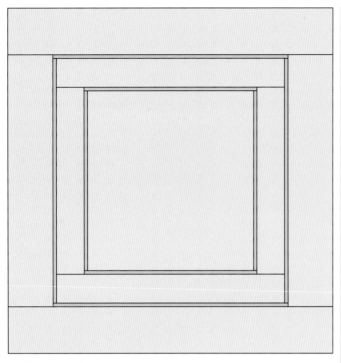

Border assembly

5. Now you're ready to do the appliqué. Nothing here is exact, just place the flowers and leaves as you like using the picture on page 16 for a guide.

6. Layer and baste. You're ready to quilt!

Quilting

First ditch-quilt all the seam-lines with a pale beige thread. Flowers are quilted close to the edges to anchor the appliquéd pieces. The leaves are given veins and surrounded by more leaves that are similar in shape to the appliquéd leaves. A vine with leaves and curls, mixing the designs from pages 50 and 51, surrounds the center flower and fills the inner border. Quilt a second row to make the vine look more like a ribbon.

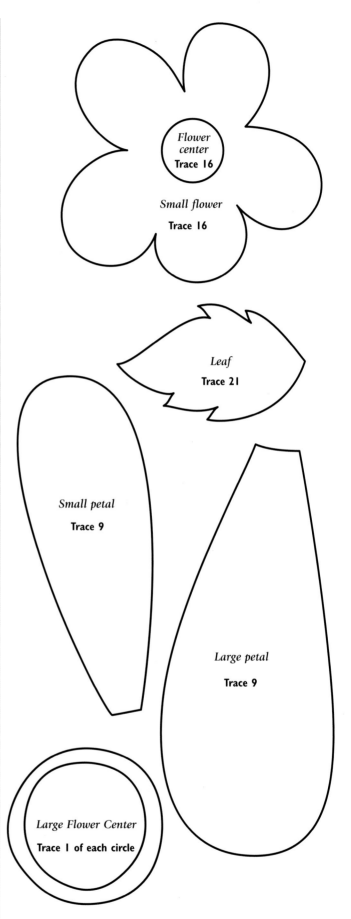

Flower center **Trace 16**

Small flower **Trace 16**

Leaf **Trace 21**

Small petal **Trace 9**

Large petal **Trace 9**

Large Flower Center **Trace 1 of each circle**

Patterns for *Poppin' Poppies* – **Enlarge 195%**

All small flowers are quilted in the same manner.

Quilting designs on *Poppin' Poppies*

Old Glory, 44" x 40", designed and quilted by the author; pieced by Maggie Hall, Volcano, California.

Fabrics

Red and beige for flag stripes—$1/2$ yard each. These
  fabrics need to be 42" wide after selvages are cut off.
Pale blue for background—$3/4$ yard
Vivid blue for star field—$1/4$ yard
Various reds, beiges, and blues for pieced border—total
  of 1 yard
Backing—1 $1/4$ yards
Cotton batting—approximately 45" x 50"
Binding—$1/2$ yard

Cutting

Beige
Cut six 2"-wide strips.

Red
Cut seven 2"-wide strips.

Vivid Blue
Cut three 2"-wide strips and from these cut seven
11"-long pieces.

Pale Blue
Cut two 6"-wide strips.
Cut four 3"-wide strips. Cut two of the 3"-wide strips
32" long. Wait to cut the two remaining lengths.

Various Reds, Beiges, and Blues
Cut 152 total 2 $1/2$" squares.

Binding
Cut five 2 $1/2$"-wide strips.

Piecing

1. Begin by sewing alternate strips of red and beige
together. Pin **carefully** and sew each row to eliminate
curving of the piece.

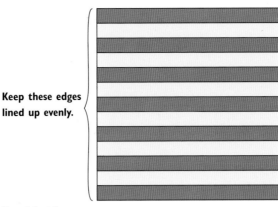

**Keep these edges
lined up evenly.**

Sew 13 strips.

2. After all thirteen strips are sewn together, starting and
ending with a red strip, sew a 6"-wide pale blue strip to
both top and bottom. Press all the seams in one direction. Now cut into twenty-one 2"-wide sections.

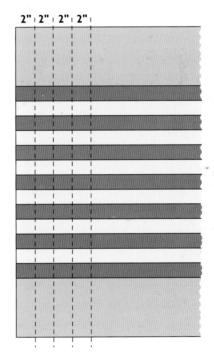

2" 2" 2" 2"

Add pale blue strips, then cut 21 sections.

3. Carefully remove the top seven red and beige stripes
and the 6" pale blue piece from **7 sections**. Then
replace these with a vivid blue 11" piece. Now sew only
the pale blue pieces to the vivid blue pieces. Press in the
same direction as in Step 2.

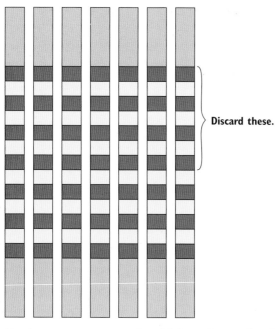

} Discard these.

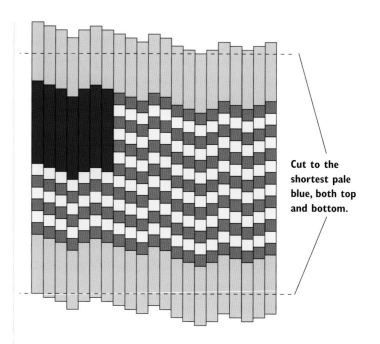

Cut to the shortest pale blue, both top and bottom.

Gently remove top seven red and beige stripes, saving the pale blue piece.

Make a very gentle wave. Cut straight across with rotary cutter.

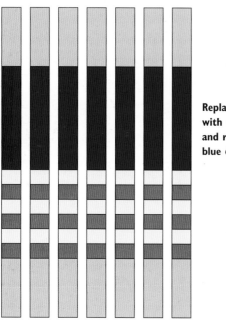

Replace discards with vivid blue and reattach pale blue 6" pieces.

5. Add the 3" x 32" pale blue strips to the top and bottom. Press seams toward border. Measure the height of your quilt top and cut the two remaining 3"-wide pale blue strips this measurement. **After** these borders are sewn on and pressed, your quilt top needs to measure an even number plus $1/2$".

6. Trim from both sides and top and bottom if you need to make any adjustments. This will make adding the squares easy. Put the piece back up on your design wall and place the $2\,1/2$" squares in a random pattern until you are pleased.

4. Using your design wall, place the sections in a "wave" pattern to your liking. Use the picture on page 20 as a guide. Then piece them together and press all the seams in one direction. Using your rotary cutter, trim the top and bottom to the shortest pale blue piece.

🌼 *Note* Keep them in a **gentle** wave without extreme movement.

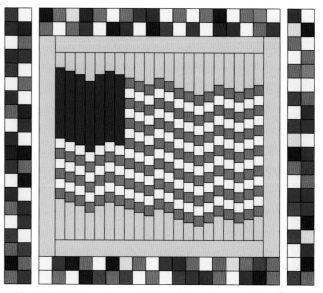

Add pale blue 3" strips on all four sides. Arrange the $2\,1/2$" squares.

7. Sew the 2 1/2" squares into strips. Press and add the strips to top and bottom, then the sides. Press.

8. Layer and baste. You're ready to quilt!

Quilting

You can quilt your quilt any way you want! I chose to ditch-quilt all the main seams with clear nylon thread.

Stars are quilted in both the pieced border squares and the vivid blue "star field." See Stars on page 53. Words of the "Pledge of Allegiance" are divided more or less equally among the four pale blue borders. Random wave-like lines follow the red and beige stripes of the flag. The background quilting is a meander (page 53) with a few stars added here and there along the way.

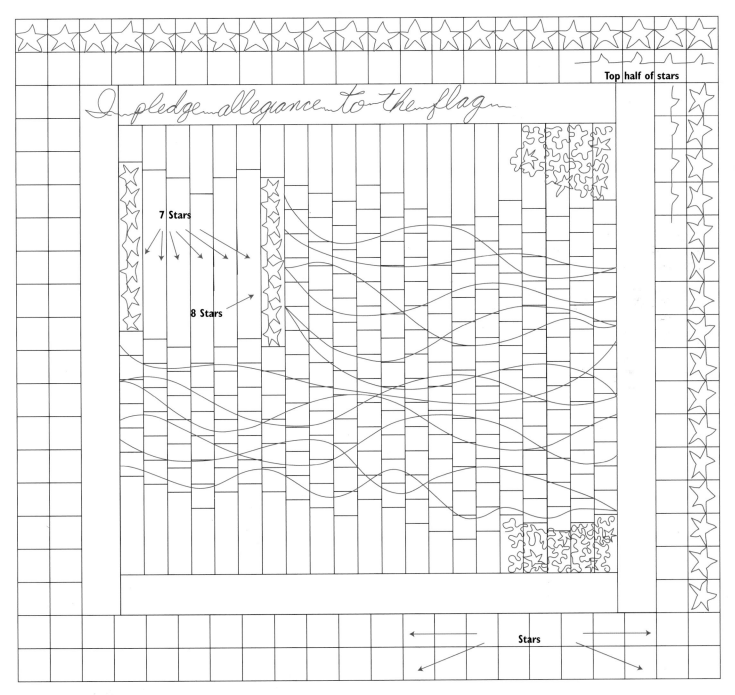

Quilting designs on *Old Glory*

Yacht Sailing, approximately 38" x 44 $^1/_2$", designed, pieced, and quilted by the author.

Fabrics

Light blue for sky—$1/2$ yard

Medium blue for water—$5/8$ yard

Inner border—$1/4$ yard

Outer border—$3/4$ yard

Yacht: $1/3$ yard for sails

$1/8$ yard for ship hull

1" x 18" strip for mast

Backing—1 $1/2$ yards

Cotton batting—approximately 42" x 49"

Binding—$1/2$ yard

Lightweight fusible webbing—1 yard

Appliqué

All designs need to be enlarged 195%. Draw designs on paper side of fusible webbing and cut out roughly—approximately $1/4$" outside your lines. Fuse these onto the wrong side of the fabrics, then cut exactly on the lines.

Cutting

Sky—Cut a 15 $1/2$"-high by 26 $1/2$"-wide piece.

Water—Cut an 18"-high by 26 $1/2$"-wide piece.

Inner border—Cut four 2"-wide strips into two 33"-long strips and two 29 $1/2$"-long strips.

Outer border—Cut four 5"-wide strips into two 36"-long strips and two 38 $1/2$"-long strips.

Binding—Cut five 2 $1/2$"-wide strips.

Piecing

1. Sew the sky and water together along the 26 $1/2$" width. Press toward the water.

2. Sew the 33 $1/2$"-long inner borders to the opposite sides of the center piece. Press toward center piece. Sew the 29 $1/2$"-long inner borders to the top and bottom. Press toward the center piece.

3. Sew the 36"-long outer borders to opposite sides of the center piece. Press toward the outer border. Sew the 38 $1/2$"-long outer borders to the top and bottom. Press toward the outer border.

4. The mast is a strip $1/2$" wide at the bottom narrowing gradually to $1/4$" wide at the top. It is easiest to fuse a 1"-wide strip of webbing to the mast fabric, then use a rotary cutter and ruler to cut the mast to size.

5. My flag was made from a small scrap of the ship hull fabric; you can use any fabric you want. Place and fuse the ship hull, mast, then the sails and flag using the picture as a guide.

6. I used a narrow machine buttonhole stitch with thread matching the various fabrics to anchor the fused pieces, but you could use the quilting stitches to do the same thing.

7. Layer and baste, then you're ready to quilt!

Quilting

Quilting designs are all included in the back of the book with the ocean/water designs on pages 54-55. Don't forget to give your yacht a name. I used a combination of my children's first names. In an effort to make the quilting design show more, I quilted the outside border of boats twice, once in yellow thread and once in red thread. You can use this double layered quilting with great effect on many large, open designs.

Sailboats on all four borders

Rope

Quilting designs on *Yacht Sailing*

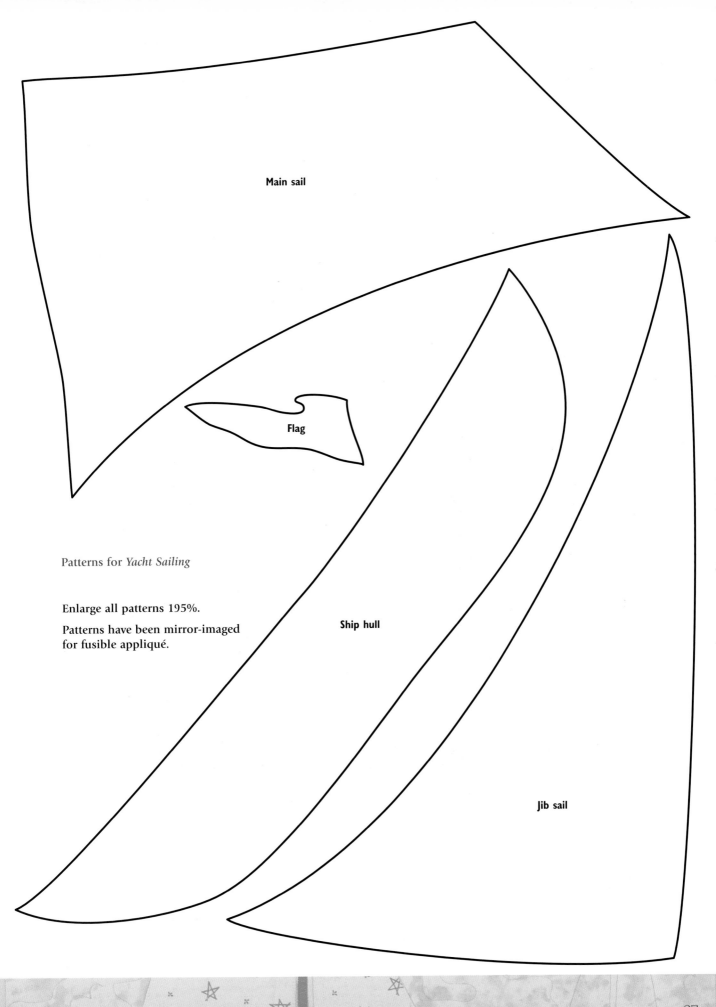

Main sail

Flag

Patterns for *Yacht Sailing*

Enlarge all patterns 195%.

Patterns have been mirror-imaged
for fusible appliqué.

Ship hull

Jib sail

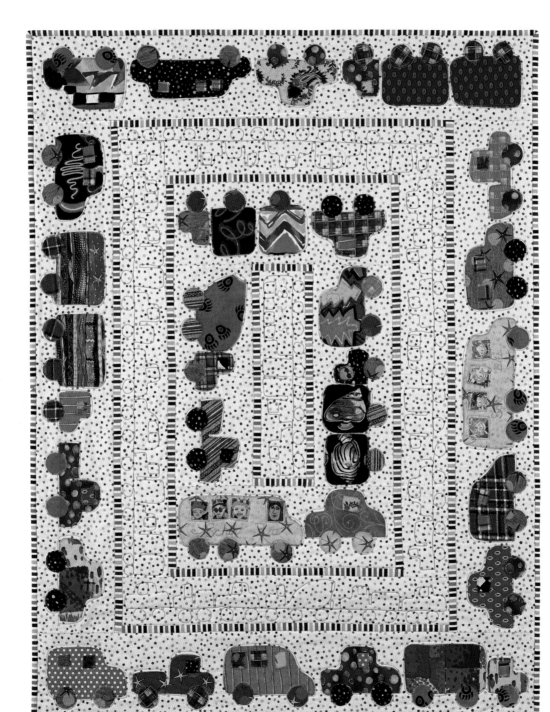

Two-Way Traffic!, approximately 36" x 48", designed, pieced, and quilted by the author.

Fabrics

Background—2 yards

Narrow stripe for inner borders and binding—$3/4$ yard

Bright colors for vehicles—scraps of 20 or more

Backing—1 $1/2$ yards

Cotton batting—approximately 52" x 40"

Lightweight fusible webbing—2 yards if 18" wide

Appliqué

All patterns need to be enlarged 195%. Using the fusible webbing, draw the shapes on the paper side, and cut out roughly $1/4$" outside the lines. Fuse these onto the wrong side of the fabric, then cut out exactly on the lines.

Cutting

Background

Cut six 6 $1/2$"-wide strips into four 37 $1/2$"-long pieces and four 17"-long pieces.

Cut five 3 $1/2$"-wide strips into one 15 $1/2$"-long piece (center), two 23 $1/2$"-long pieces and two 29 $1/2$"-long pieces.

Narrow Stripe

Cut eight 1"-wide strips into two 4 $1/2$"-long pieces, two 15 $1/2$"-long pieces, two 17 $1/2$"-long pieces, two 28 $1/2$"-long pieces, two 24 $1/2$"-long pieces, and two 35 $1/2$"-long pieces.

Cut five 2 $1/2$"-wide strips for binding.

Note It is much easier to fuse and buttonhole stitch around the edges of the appliqué shapes before you sew the appliquéd background strips to the quilt top. So, the strips are cut with a little extra allowing for shrinkage. The lengths in the cutting instruction include the bit extra. Appliqué the vehicles, then sew the whole quilt top together.

Use a variety of shapes, and place them to fill the strips. Appliqué on the 6 $1/2$"-wide pieces **only**. Shorten some of the trucks, or cars, etc. to make them fit just right. Remember nothing here needs to be an exact fit.

Choose the SUV's, cars, trucks, etc. that you like and fill the strips leaving enough room at top, bottom, and both ends for sewing them together.

I used brightly colored variegated thread to buttonhole stitch around all the pieces—including the windows and wheels. The quilt could be color-coordinated to match a child's room or a baby's layette, but scraps of brightly colored fabrics make it really fun!!

Piecing

1. Sew the 15 $1/2$"-long narrow stripe pieces to the sides of the 3 $1/2$" x 15 $1/2$" background piece. The narrow stripe is **always** pressed toward itself. Sew the 4 $1/2$"-long narrow stripe pieces to the top and bottom. Press toward the narrow stripe.

2. Trim the 6 $1/2$" x 17" pieces with the vehicles appliquéd to be 6 $1/2$" x 16 $1/2$". Sew two to the sides. Press toward the narrow stripe. Sew the remaining two to the top and bottom. Press toward the narrow stripe.

3. Sew the 28 $1/2$"-long narrow stripe pieces to the sides. Press. Sew the 17 $1/2$"-long narrow stripe pieces to the top and bottom. Press.

4. Next, sew the 3 $1/2$" x 29 $1/2$"-long pieces (nothing appliquéd on them) to the sides. Press toward the narrow stripe. Sew the 3 $1/2$" x 23 $1/2$" pieces to the top and bottom. Press.

5. Sew the 35 $1/2$"-long narrow stripe pieces to the sides. Press. Sew the 24 $1/2$"-long narrow stripe pieces to the top and bottom. Press.

6. Trim the last round of appliquéd 6 $1/2$" x 37 $1/2$" strips to 6 $1/2$" x 36 $1/2$". Sew to the sides. Press toward the narrow stripe. Sew the remaining two to the top and bottom. Press.

7. You're ready to layer, baste, and quilt.

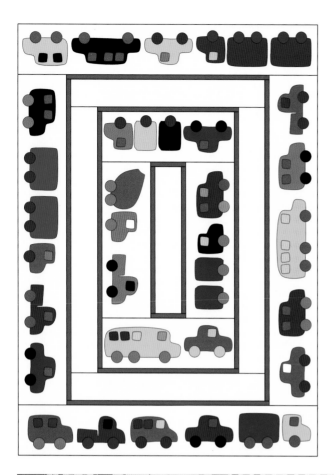

Quilting

The appliquéd cars, trucks, etc. are facing one direction and the quilted vehicles are facing the opposite direction—hence the name *Two-Way Traffic*! I did the quilting using a dark solid-color 30-weight cotton thread so it would really show—but it would look great done in the variegated thread as well. The open borders were quilted with the cars, trucks, buses, etc. designs from page 57.

All the seam lines were ditch-quilted first with white thread. All the vehicles including their windows and wheels were outlined (ditched) with variegated thread.

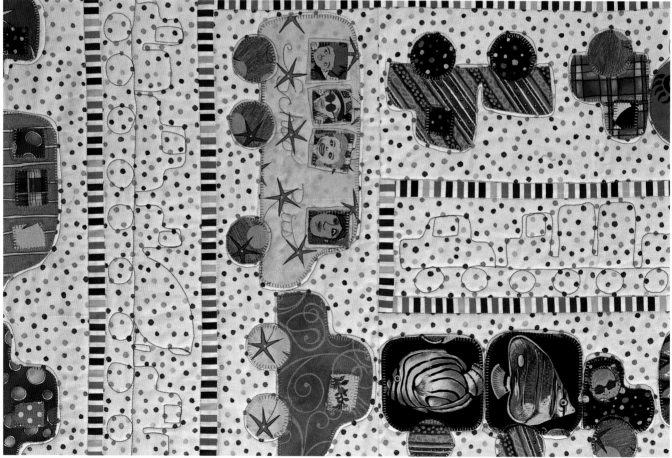

Detail of *Two-Way Traffic!*

School Bus

School Bus

School Bus

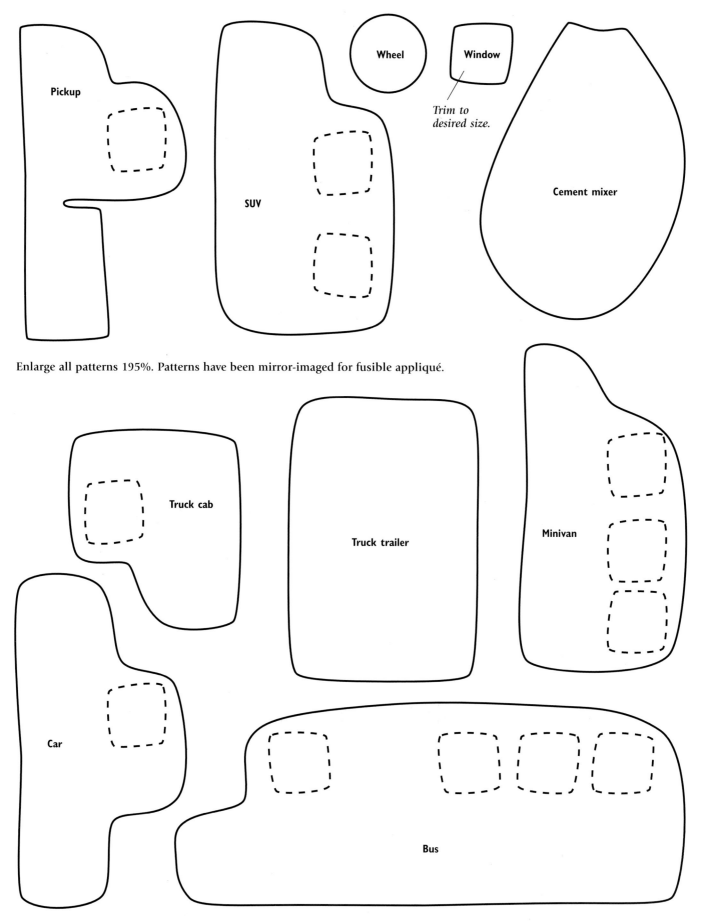

Pickup

SUV

Wheel

Window

Trim to
desired size.

Cement mixer

Enlarge all patterns 195%. Patterns have been mirror-imaged for fusible appliqué.

Truck cab

Truck trailer

Minivan

Car

Bus

Patterns for *Two-Way Traffic!*

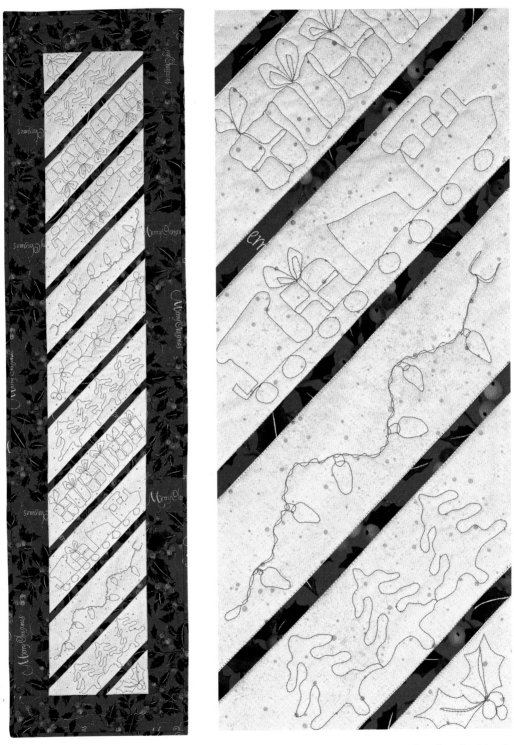

Merry Christmas Table Runner, 17" x 56", pieced by Maggie Hall, Volcano, California; designed and quilted by the author.

Fabrics

Red—1 yard
Beige—³/₄ yard
Backing—21" x 60" long piece
Cotton batting—approximately 21" x 60"

Cutting

Red

Cut five 1"-wide strips.
Cut four 3 ¹/₂"-wide strips for border.
Cut four 2 ¹/₂"-wide strips for binding.

Beige

Cut five 3 ¹/₂"-wide strips.

Piecing

1. Sew together pairs of beige strips and 1"-wide red strips. Sew paired strips together in a 3 ¹/₂" "step-down" fashion. After all the strips are sewn together, press the seams toward narrow red strips.

2. Using a 24" ruler and a rotary cutter, cut one end at a 45° angle. Then cut two sections that are 12" wide at the same angle.

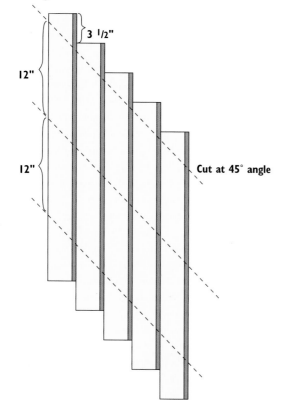

3. Sew these sections together and press the seam toward the red narrow strip.

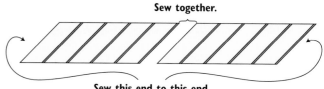

Sew together.

Sew this end to this end.

4. Now sew the ends together to make a circle, and gently press the seam toward the narrow red strip of fabric.

5. To make one long rectangle, carefully draw a chalk line straight across and cut on this line with a scissors.

Chalk line and cutting line

6. Sew the short ends of the 3 ¹/₂"-wide border strips together on the diagonal into one length. Then measure the length of the runner and cut the side borders. Sew the side borders on first. Measure the width of the runner and cut the top and bottom borders to this length and sew to the ends of the runner.

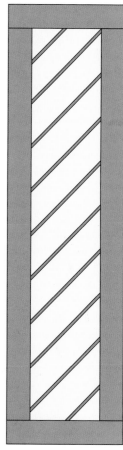

Adding borders

7. Layer and baste, and you're ready to quilt.

Quilting

All the seam lines were ditch-quilted first with clear nylon thread. The Christmas designs all appear on pages 58-59. The train design was slightly altered from the one on page 57 to have packages instead of being a passenger-type car.

Quilting designs on *Merry Christmas Table Runner*

Sampler Quilts

Most of us start our quilting hobby with one or more sampler quilts. This chapter is devoted to easy, no-mark quilting designs suitable for a variety of sampler blocks.

Once again, I recommend that you "grid" quilt the piece before doing the decorative quilting. Grid the main body of the piece and then ditch-quilt the inner and outer borders if desired.

Beverly's quilt is a classic sampler quilt with soft colors and a floral theme. All the major seams were ditch-quilted first. The blocks, set on point, were quilted with simple designs of leaves and flowers. The large setting triangles, corner triangles and borders were quilted with feathers (see page 60).

Bev's Pastel Fantasy, 68" x 100", pieced by Beverly Linklater, Volcano, California; quilted by the author.

All four corners quilted the same

Each setting triangle quilted the same

Leaves

Feathers all the way around

Quilting designs on *Bev's Pastel Fantasy*

Stars and More Stars, 56" x 80", pieced by Maggie Hall, Volcano, California; setting design and quilting by the author.

A great collection of traditional star blocks set on point with more stars on the border and two really large setting stars in the lattice. Quilting included ditching just the large setting stars and the borders. While I was ditch-quilting the borders, I quilted the stars in the background on the borders at the same time. Quilting also included a row of red quilted stars across the background in the four corners and meander with stars and moons in all the background, outlining here and there, and stars everywhere! (See the stars on page 53).

Quilting designs on *Stars and More Stars*

Summer Beach Houses, 40" x 51", pieced by Diana McClun, Walnut Creek, California, and Laura Nownes, Pleasant Hill, California; quilted by the author.

Summer Beach Houses is one of a series of quilts appearing in Diana and Laura's upcoming book. It provided a great canvas for water and other aquatic quilting themes. Note the seaweed quilted on the borders…this is just a long, skinny, rounded leaf with a "bump" along the way with starts and stops from the border or from the ditch. The tiny vine curls around the entire fence. Also included are a huge sun and clouds in the sky, a cypress tree in one of the yards, and rocks in another, and starfish in the "water" at the bottom of the quilt.

Quilted the same as the opposite border.

Houses are all quilted the same.

Quilting designs on *Summer Beach Houses*

Cat House Too, 42" x 66", pieced by Freddy Moran, Orinda, California; quilted by the author.

This quilt includes a different quilting design for each of the houses, often depending on the fabric choices to influence the design: a guitar on the roof of a house with guitar fabric and a giant set of lips on the house with lip fabric on the roof. The border fabric is a collection of whimsical cats and the quilting in the fabric surrounding the houses is sprinkled with similar cat faces quilted double-lined in red thread. Two of Freddy's house blocks are used in this quilt, set with large spaces (perfect for quilting) in the background. All the blocks and little black borders were ditch-quilted first.

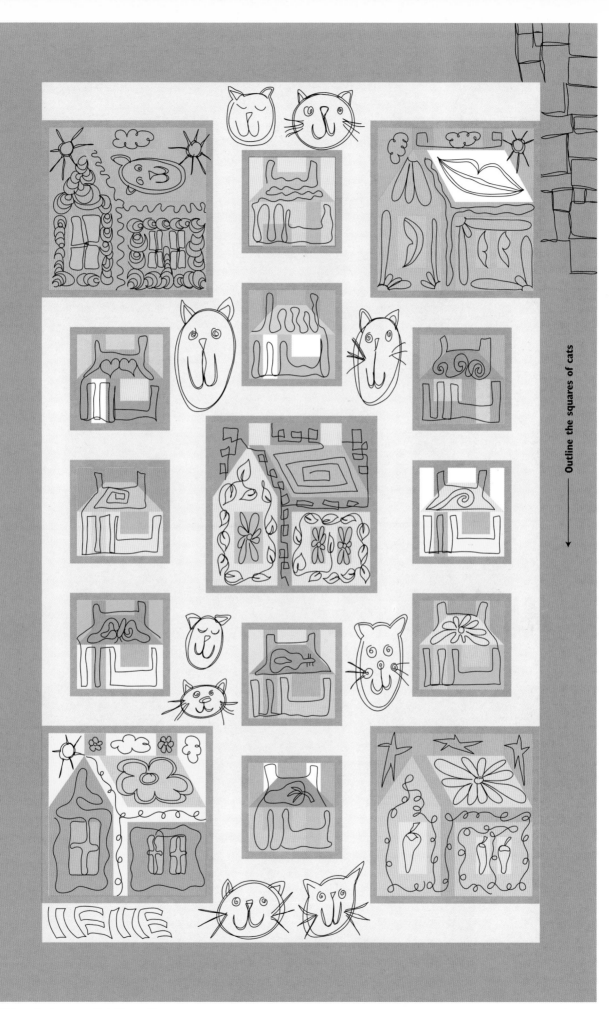

Quilting designs on *Cat House Too*

Combined Efforts, 70" x 90", pieced by Margaret J. Miller, Woodinville, Washington; Maggie Hall, Volcano, California; and the author, using Margaret Miller's *Smashing Sets*-style. The quilt includes original blocks designed by Diana McClun; quilted by the author.

Only a portion of the quilt is diagrammed; the pansy theme is worked throughout the quilt, with all pansies quilted the same. The border is quilted in a vine combining an echoed pansy and leaves. Inner setting strips include an uneven cable and "curls and sticks." The designs can be found on pages 51 and 62.

Quilting designs on
Combined Efforts

Christmas Heart Lights, 74" square. From the book of the same name written and published by Susie Robbins of Vallejo, California; pieced by Maggie Hall, Volcano, California; quilted by the author.

Quilted with the variety of Christmas designs found in Chapter 8, pages 58-59, including packages all the way around the border. This quilt has many open spaces that can showcase quilting designs such as large gift packages and the pine bough done in the background.

All the holly
leaves are veined.

All the pinwheels are
quilted the same.

Packages on all four sides

Quilting designs on *Christmas Heart Lights*

Designs

Starts and stops are not fun, and can be more noticeable than desired. Look for and work on developing continuous-line designs. Many patterns designed for hand quilting can be altered slightly to be continuous and easier to use for machine quilting.

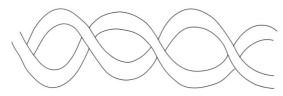

Hand quilting design

Machine quilting design

Marking or Not Marking

Most quilters do not enjoy marking quilting designs, nor do they enjoy finding the exact-sized template or the right marking tool for the fabric. Then removing any remaining visible lines after quilting can also be troublesome. All of these can be frustrating and cause us to give up and move on to another project.

Forget all the marking, and move on to fun, whimsical, fast, not perfect designs that don't have to be marked and yet look wonderful. These designs will also add personality to your piece and are **easy** to learn. You need to try to erase the mindset that says quilting designs have

to be perfect to look good. For instance, if you quilt twelve stars and eleven are perfect and one is crooked, the crooked one looks wrong. But if all twelve stars are slightly crooked then they all look good and the slight imperfections are part of the design.

Remember the five categories from Chapter 6, page 15? I have developed a number of designs in each category that are all easy to quilt and **do not** need to be marked. Remember that most of these designs can be chained together or grouped, or will stand alone, giving you more variations.

How Do I Quilt **That** Quilt?

After quilting so many different quilts during the last ten years, I have a formula for deciding just how a quilt should be quilted. After deciding which of the five categories a quilt is in, I then pick the designs based on overall direction, style, and general movement—vertical or horizontal, diagonal, or circular basic plan—of the piece. Using a paper and pencil, you can probably sketch more designs based on the quilt patterns given in the book for quilting each quilt you have. Some of the fabrics used may have wonderful bugs, bows, animals, flowers, leaves or other designs that you can "draw with your needle" to make quilting designs for your quilt.

Designs You Don't Have to Mark

Now here's where the fun begins! Here are designs for each of the categories and with just a bit of practice you can quilt them without marking. Really! You'll probably be quilting on printed fabric so the "camouflage factor" will help hide any small irregularities (they're **not** mistakes).

Don't say "but I'm not an artist" or that you couldn't draw your way out of a box. I'm not an artist, and can't draw a horse or cow or a dinosaur without help, but I have learned to use books, fabrics, nature, and all sorts of pictures for inspiration for quilting designs. Look around you at the basic designs and lines, curves and waves, tree branches, rock formations, leaves and flowers in your environment. You will discover ideas that can all be used for inspiration for quilting designs. I used a cookbook for the designs on one quilt. The small drawings in the fish section were perfect inspiration for quilting designs in an Ocean Waves quilt.

Unless you are experienced and very comfortable with free-motion machine quilting, you need to practice the designs before beginning to quilt on the quilt top that you've spent months piecing or appliquéing.

Getting Ready to Play

Baste together one half yard of muslin or similar colored fabric, cotton batting and backing with safety pins. Use a neutral color thread and begin just playing—drawing with the needle. This is not going into the Smithsonian so you can make all the mistakes, starts, stops, and ugly stitching you want. Just **play**! Start with the easiest—a single leaf or two, and go through the pages of designs trying anything and everything.

🌸 *Tip* *Don't try to make them perfect! Small variations or imperfections won't be noticeable, but part of the plan. After a bit of practice, you will find that the small mistakes or errors will become part of the charm and personality of the quilt. Also remember that when quilted on printed fabrics, your irregularities—**not mistakes**—don't show! It takes just a small amount of practice—and remember to have **fun**!*

Designs

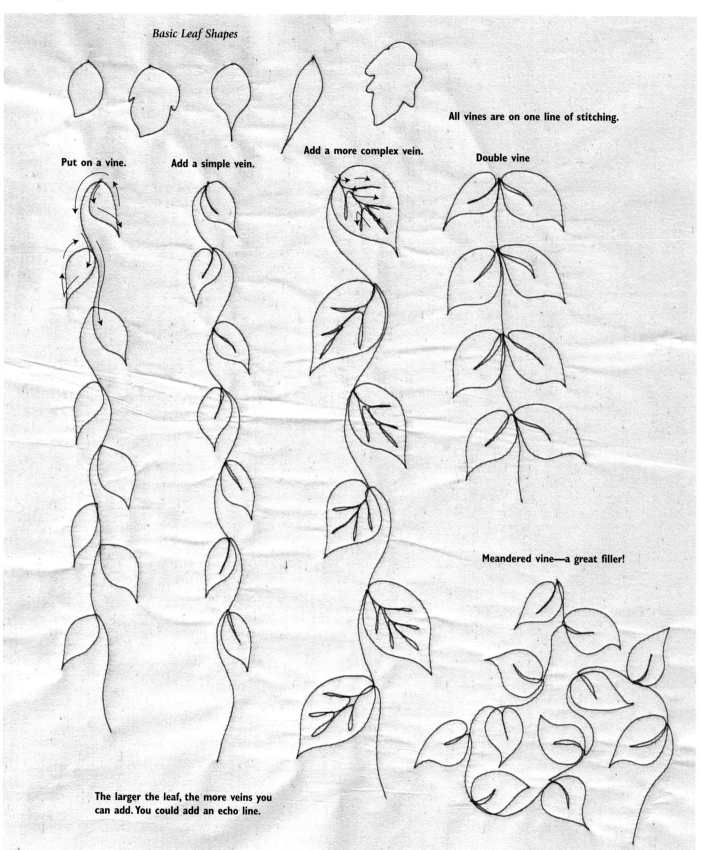

Basic Leaf Shapes

All vines are on one line of stitching.

Put on a vine.

Add a simple vein.

Add a more complex vein.

Double vine

Meandered vine—a great filler!

The larger the leaf, the more veins you can add. You could add an echo line.

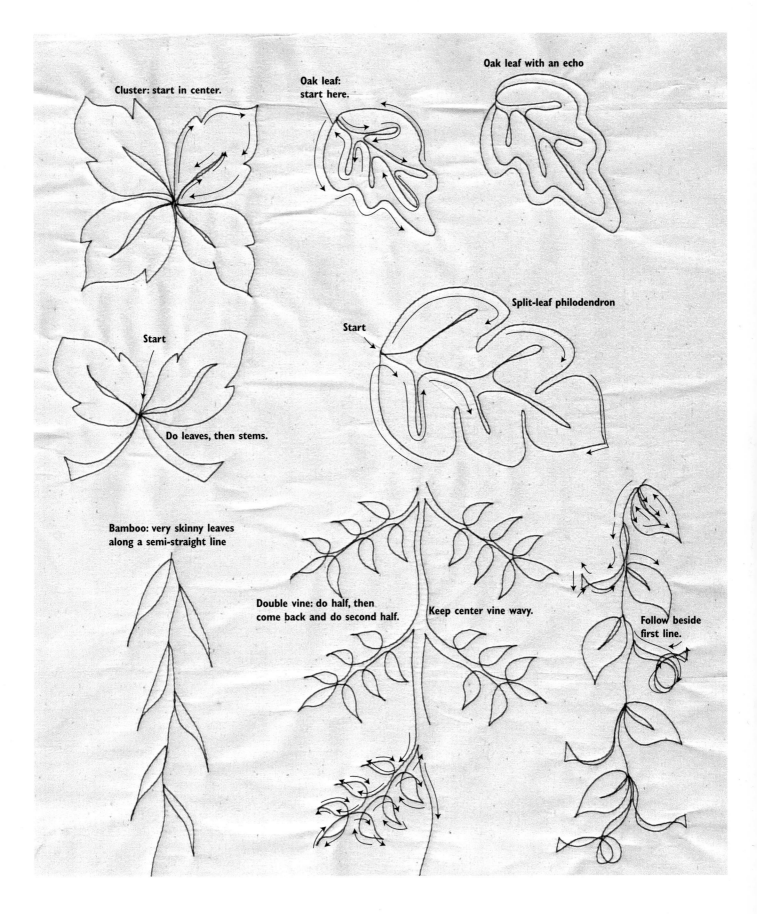

Cluster: start in center.

Oak leaf: start here.

Oak leaf with an echo

Start

Do leaves, then stems.

Split-leaf philodendron

Start

Bamboo: very skinny leaves along a semi-straight line

Double vine: do half, then come back and do second half.

Keep center vine wavy.

Follow beside first line.

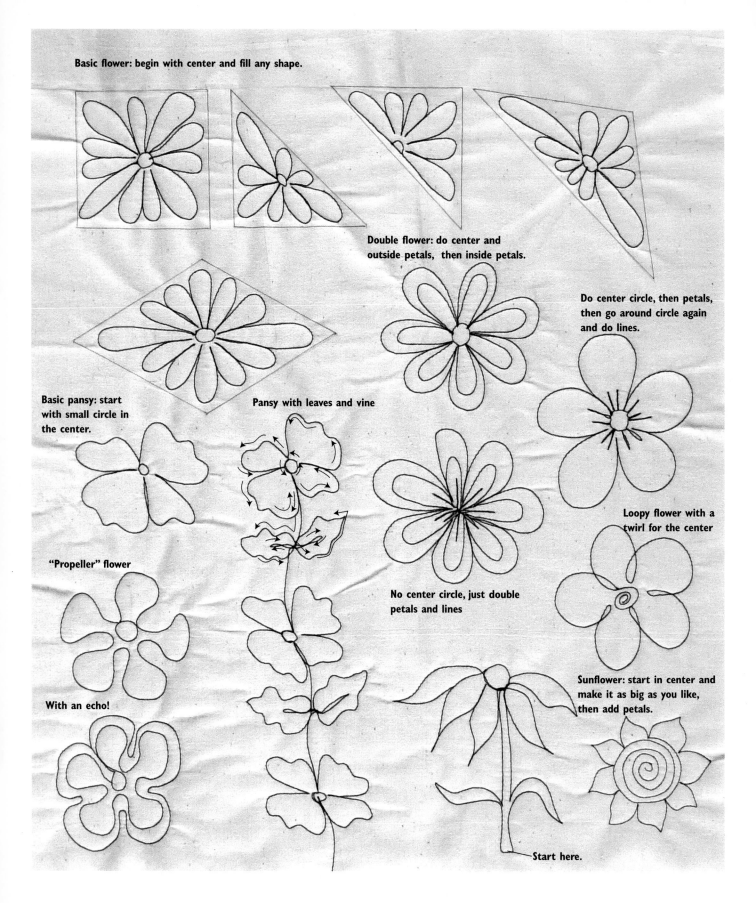

Basic flower: begin with center and fill any shape.

Double flower: do center and outside petals, then inside petals.

Do center circle, then petals, then go around circle again and do lines.

Basic pansy: start with small circle in the center.

Pansy with leaves and vine

"Propeller" flower

No center circle, just double petals and lines

Loopy flower with a twirl for the center

With an echo!

Sunflower: start in center and make it as big as you like, then add petals.

Start here.

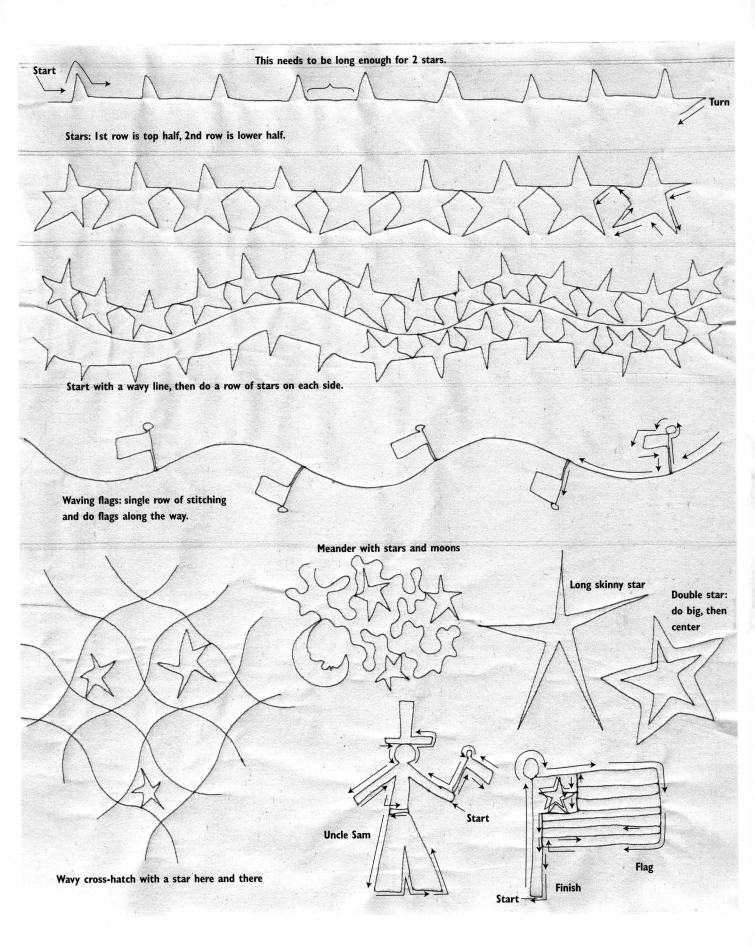

This needs to be long enough for 2 stars.

Start

Turn

Stars: 1st row is top half, 2nd row is lower half.

Start with a wavy line, then do a row of stars on each side.

Waving flags: single row of stitching and do flags along the way.

Meander with stars and moons

Long skinny star

Double star: do big, then center

Wavy cross-hatch with a star here and there

Uncle Sam

Start

Start

Finish

Flag

Start

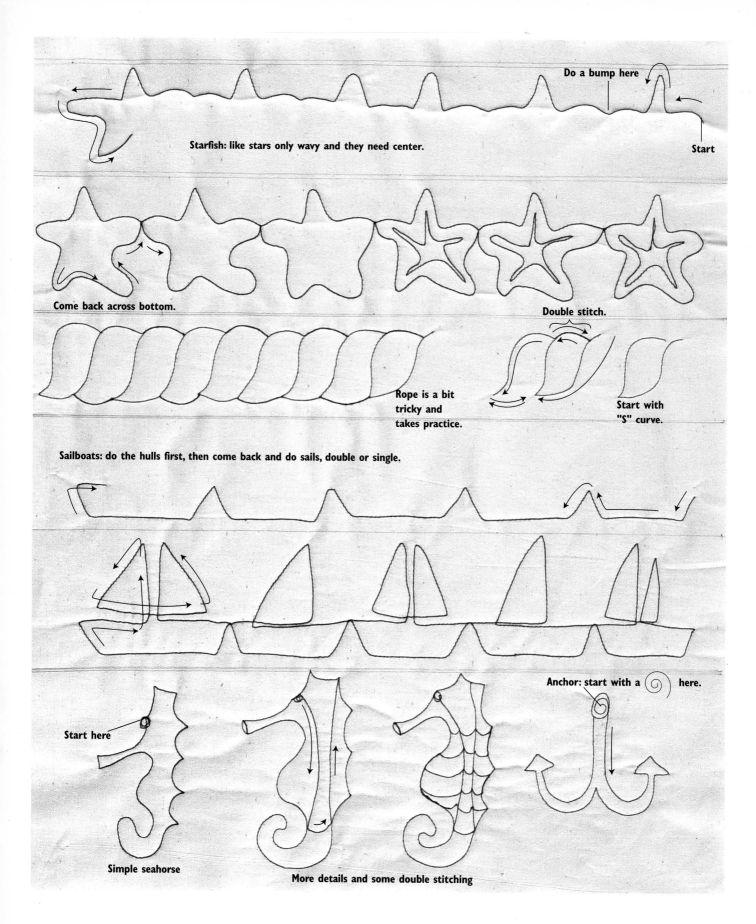

Do a bump here

Start

Starfish: like stars only wavy and they need center.

Come back across bottom.

Double stitch.

Rope is a bit tricky and takes practice.

Start with "S" curve.

Sailboats: do the hulls first, then come back and do sails, double or single.

Anchor: start with a ⟳ **here.**

Start here

Simple seahorse

More details and some double stitching

Waves start here.

Waves that overlap, big and little

Long meander that looks like water

Add fish along the way.

Rows of fish start here.

Come back along lower half.

Slightly more detailed row of fish, add fins and eye along the way.

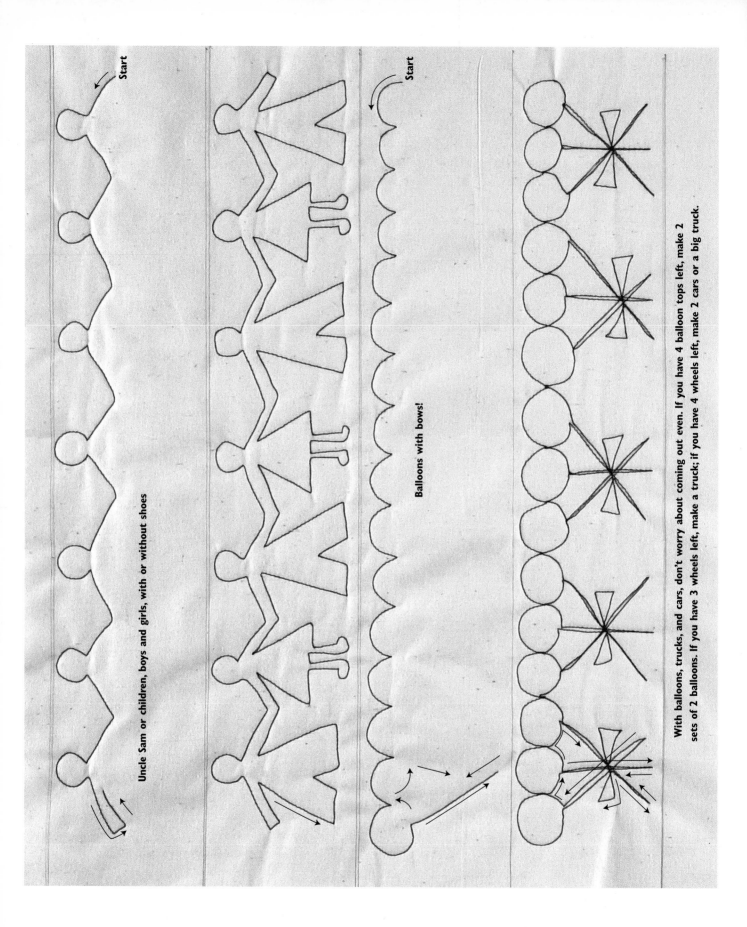

Start

Uncle Sam or children, boys and girls, with or without shoes

Start

Balloons with bows!

With balloons, trucks, and cars, don't worry about coming out even. If you have 4 balloon tops left, make 2 sets of 2 balloons. If you have 3 wheels left, make a truck; if you have 4 wheels left, make 2 cars or a big truck.

Cars, trucks: just make circles on a line, then come back across with the cabs.

Start

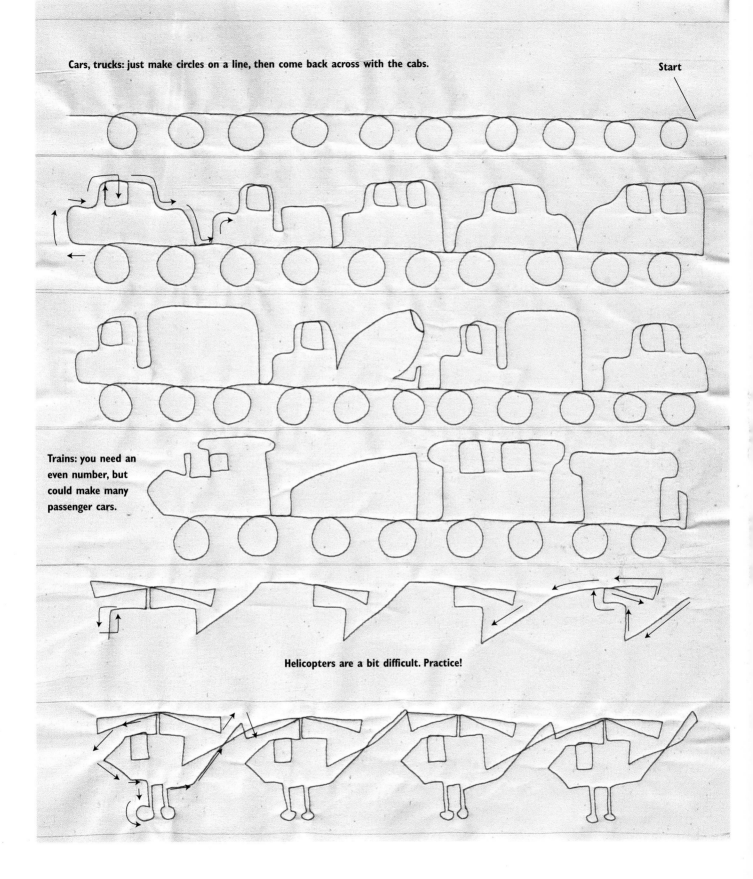

Trains: you need an even number, but could make many passenger cars.

Helicopters are a bit difficult. Practice!

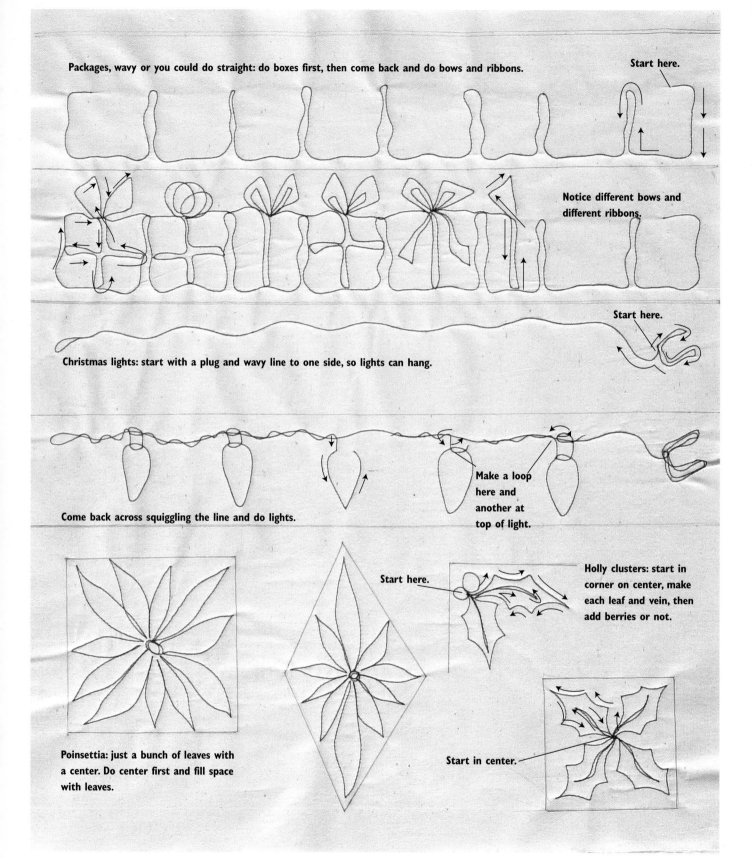

Packages, wavy or you could do straight: do boxes first, then come back and do bows and ribbons.

Start here.

Notice different bows and different ribbons.

Start here.

Christmas lights: start with a plug and wavy line to one side, so lights can hang.

Come back across squiggling the line and do lights.

Make a loop here and another at top of light.

Start here.

Holly clusters: start in corner on center, make each leaf and vein, then add berries or not.

Poinsettia: just a bunch of leaves with a center. Do center first and fill space with leaves.

Start in center.

Holly: first line is wavy line down the center.

Second line is one half of leaves.

Third line is second half of leaves and berries.

Wavy trees: start across the base and keep line wavy, then come back across top.

Quilt enough length here for two trees.

Straight trees: more or less straight lines, different heights.

Single package: quilt outside edge, the bow, then ribbon ends.

Start here.

Start here.

Bells

Feathers: begin with a tear shape, then rotate side to side.

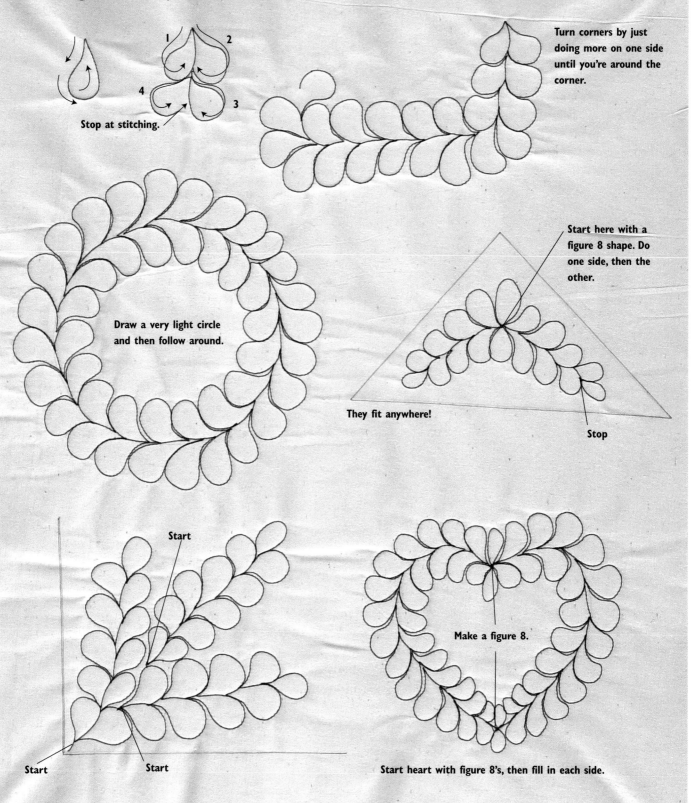

1 2

4 3

Stop at stitching.

Turn corners by just doing more on one side until you're around the corner.

Draw a very light circle and then follow around.

Start here with a figure 8 shape. Do one side, then the other.

They fit anywhere!

Stop

Start

Start

Start

Make a figure 8.

Start heart with figure 8's, then fill in each side.

Echo

Meander

Overlap meander

Meander with weeds

Square maze

Meander with clouds

Round maze

Bricks, shingles, wood

A great background filler!

Backgrounds or fillers

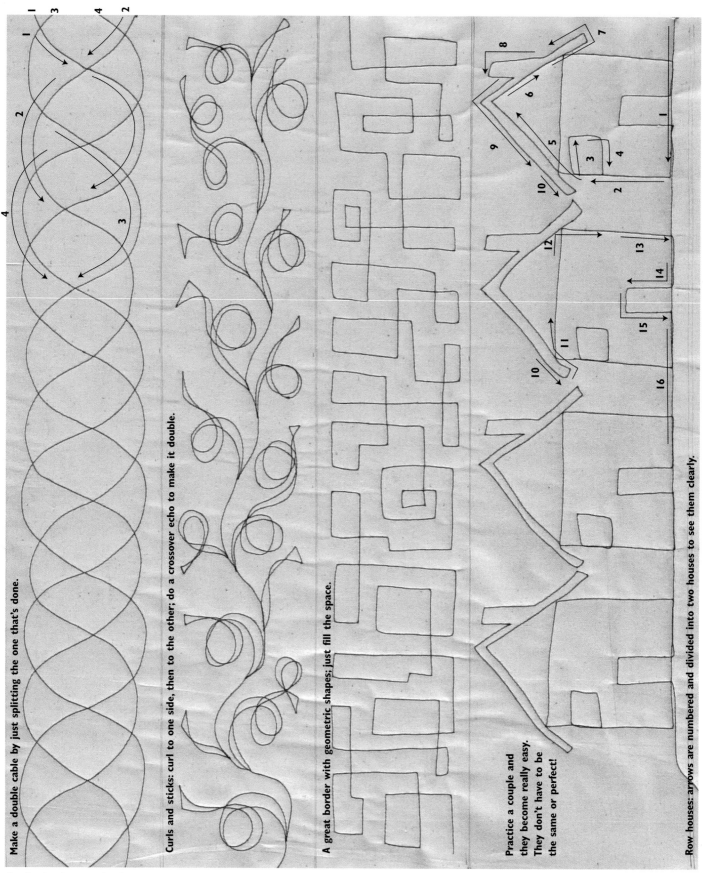

Make a double cable by just splitting the one that's done.

Curls and sticks: curl to one side, then to the other; do a crossover echo to make it double.

A great border with geometric shapes; just fill the space.

Practice a couple and they become really easy. They don't have to be the same or perfect!

Row houses: arrows are numbered and divided into two houses to see them clearly.

Border Designs: 4 simple ones